AIDAN STOREY

ON ANGELS' WINGS

Adapted from *Angels of Divine Light*
(Transworld Ireland, 2010)

Aidan Storey was born and raised in Dublin. He has become established as one of the leading Irish psychics, Angel therapists and Angel readers. He specialises in helping people to deal with issues that prevent them from embarking on a journey to enlightenment. Visit www.angelicireland.com for more. All royalties from the Irish sales of the Open Door series go to a charity of the author's choice. *On Angels' Wings* royalties go to ISPCC (Irish Society for the Prevention of Cruelty to Children), 29 Lower Baggot Street, Dublin 2.

NEW ISLAND *Open Door*

ON ANGELS' WINGS
First published 2011
by New Island
2 Brookside
Dundrum Road
Dublin 14

www.newisland.ie

Copyright © 2011 Aidan Storey

The right of Aidan Storey to be identified as the author of this work has been asserted by him in accordance with the Copyright, Designs and Patents Act, 1988

Adapted and reproduced with permission of Transworld Ireland, from *Angels of Divine Light*, © Aidan Storey, 2010.

A CIP catalogue record for this book is available from the British Library

ISBN: 978-1-84840-100-6

New Island receives financial assistance from The Arts Council (An Chomhairle Ealaíon), Dublin, Ireland.

Typeset by Mariel Deegan
Printed by Drukarnia Skleniarz
Cover design by Artmark

10 9 8 7 6 5 4 3 2 1

Dear Reader,

On behalf of myself and the other contributing authors, I would like to welcome you to the seventh Open Door series. We hope that you enjoy the books and that reading becomes a lasting pleasure in your life.

Warmest wishes,

Patricia Scanlan.

Patricia Scanlan
Series Editor

THE OPEN DOOR SERIES IS DEVELOPED WITH THE ASSISTANCE OF THE CITY OF DUBLIN VOCATIONAL EDUCATION COMMITTEE.

Contents

The Awakening

Suffer little children to come unto me.

Chapter 1

O Angel of God, my guardian dear
To whom God's love commits me here
Ever this day be at my side
To light and guard to rule and guide.
Amen.

This prayer always reminds me of my mother. It was the first prayer my mam taught me. It is one of my earliest memories. Every night she tucked me into bed and gave me my goodnight kiss. She'd whisper in a gentle voice, "Did you say your Guardian Angel prayer?" She would sit or stand by my bed and recite it very slowly with me. She'd remind me to replace the word "day" with "night". Sometimes she would tell me the story of my Guardian Angel. I loved when she did that, and never tired of hearing it.

"Before you came to live with me, Aidan, you lived with Holy God up in the sky. Because you were small, Holy God kept you safe and sound in His pocket. One very warm night when we were all asleep, He took you out of his pocket and left you on the back doorstep. He sent an Angel with you to keep you safe. I found you very early the next morning. That Angel is still with you. He is your Guardian Angel. He's your best friend. He will watch over you and keep you safe always. His name is also Aidan," she would say with a big smile. I felt so important. Imagine having an Angel with the same name as you? "Your Guardian Angel always has the same name as yourself," Mam said. "Mine is called

Kathleen." I loved this story. It always made me feel safe before I went to sleep. And, of course, I had no reason to believe any differently. You see, from a very young age I could see Angels. They were always by my side.

There were always many Angels. I don't know why I never told Mam or anyone else about these beautiful beings. I thought everyone could see them. I suppose at the age of four or five I thought that once you recited this beautiful prayer they just appeared.

Chapter 2

I was born in 1958. I was the youngest of seven children. I was a little spoiled and very well looked after by my older sisters and brothers. My father, also called Aidan, worked for Guinness driving lorries. He enjoyed his job. He worked hard, like many others of that era. The hours were long. He would often have to stay away overnight if he were on a long run. This would happen quite often, mainly coming up to Christmas when the brewery was busy.

My father was a stocky man with a very straight walk and an air of authority. He was the main breadwinner in the house. He handed the housekeeping money over to my mother every Thursday night. We got sweets and chocolate that night and our own pocket money. The amount depended on how old we were. I, being the youngest, always got the least. Payday was a great day in our house.

Dad was a very devout Catholic. He carried out his Church duties with great faith and without question. Whatever the priest said was law. But he also believed in ghosts and the banshee and the tapping of the passing soul on the window. He told us how he saw the banshee outside his house shortly before his own father died.

She sat on the wall, a slight figure of a woman dressed in black. She sat combing her long hair, crying and wailing like a trapped cat. The sound could be heard for miles.

Dad claimed he saw the banshee many times just before someone died. He also talked about the three taps on the window he'd heard a few times. This happened when someone close passed away. The spirit would tap on the window to say goodbye on their final journey. I know for sure this took place. Every time he heard the knock on the window we always got news that someone had passed over. This gift has passed on to me. I always get three taps on the window when loved ones pass over.

Dad was born in 1919 and grew up in Wexford on his father's small farm. He was the youngest of six children. His mother was the local midwife. He came to Dublin in his late teens and went straight into Power's distillery. After some time he went to work for Guinness. He lived for a short time with my mother's parents. That is where my mam and dad met. They fell in love, and got married.

My father was not that easy to get on with. He was the nicest and quietest of men when he had no drink in him. When he was drunk, it was a different story. He drank hard and was quite aggressive when he had taken alcohol. You didn't dare have any conversation with him when he was in this kind of state. He wasn't a bad man, but he was difficult to be around sometimes. I was a little nervous of him, as a child.

Dad became very ill during his last couple of years. It was at that stage I got to know him better. He had his own troubles to deal with. His childhood was difficult, but he did not want to discuss his past with anyone. He drank to block it out. Men were not allowed to ask for help in those days. You were just expected to get on with it. That was what he did. But he got bitter and angry as time went on and he turned to alcohol.

He was a troubled man and I'm sorry that I couldn't have the kind of relationship with him that I had with my mother. Now, with the help of the Angels, I've been given the gift of love and compassion for him. Sadly, I never really got to know my father.

He was very distant, even with Mam. My bond was much more with her. I now know that, in his own way, Dad loved me. I'm glad he's at peace.

Chapter 3

My mother, on the other hand, was very loving and was always there when we needed her. She was a woman of her time. She worked in the home and cooked and cleaned from early in the morning until late at night. With so many children to care for, she never seemed to sit down. She always had a kind word or a smile for everyone. Mam was a very straight-talking lady, but she was very caring. She was very highly thought of in the neighbourhood. She would do a good turn for anybody, day or night.

My mother was born in the Liberties, the oldest part of Dublin. At the age of six she went to live in Mount Brown, just beside what is now St James's Hospital. Her father also worked for Guinness and her mother was a cook. My mother was the oldest of seven children. She was a Wexford woman trapped inside a Dublin woman's body. She loved the country and spent most of her teens and early twenties in Wexford with relations. It was felt she was not strong and needed the fresh air.

She was a tailor by trade and served her time in the local tailoring factories around Dublin. She loved sewing. She made clothes for all of us when we were young. She also made clothes for our cousins and the neighbours. Give Mam material or an old dress, and in no time she would have made something for one of us. She was gifted with her hands. She also took in home sewing from time to time, to make a few extra pounds. She sewed into the night and, as a child, I often fell asleep to the comforting sound of the machine. She too was a devout

Catholic and went to Mass every Sunday and any time she could during the week. She did a lot of charity work and never looked for any recognition in return.

I always felt Mam had great healing powers, but it was only as I grew older and began to develop my own that I realised she had a very healing energy. People with problems were drawn to her. She always gave good, sound advice. Although she loved the Church, she was never blinded by it. She used to say, "A good turn is far better than any praying or going to Mass." She didn't always agree with what the priests and bishops had to say. She'd say, "Don't mind those priests. They don't know everything. God has the last word." This was her firm belief.

My mother gave birth to eight children: five girls and three boys. The firstborn, a girl, died a few hours after birth. She was taken away from my mother a couple of hours later and buried in the grave of the Angels in

Glasnevin. There was no counselling in those days. She was sent home and advised to have another baby as soon as possible. She never forgot her little girl and spoke of her often. As I gained more knowledge from the Angels, I was told why sometimes babies return to God so soon after birth, or why sometimes they are miscarried. Later in the book we'll come back to this and I will pass on I was told.

My mother had time for all of us, not easy as a mother of seven very different children. She always said that she had to love us all in different ways because we were all individuals. This she did superbly. It was from her I learned about unconditional love, the ultimate goal of every soul who undertakes the human journey.

Chapter 4

We lived in Kilmainham in a terraced house on the main road between Mount Brown and Kilmainham. The area was mainly working class. Most of our neighbours worked in the local hospitals, factories and, of course, Guinness.

We never had a lock on the door; it was always on the latch. We never had to take a key with us. Everyone who knew us just let themselves in. It was very common then, and it didn't matter if there was no one at home. It was safe and nobody took anything without asking.

We had very good neighbours. Mam had lived in the area all her life and knew most of the locals. Many of them had been her friends since childhood. Like herself, they hadn't moved away when they had married. People didn't seem to go far from where they grew up in those days: they stayed close to their parents. So the neighbourhood was a friendly one.

Up the road, just about six doors to our right, was the local paper mill, and on the left of us was the local corner shop, Camac Stores. Beside that was a creamery. A few sewing factories employed many of the young girls in the area. The Union, as St James's was once known, was the local hospital. It was a maternity as well as a general hospital in those days. At the time I was born it was known as St Kevin's. Many people of my mother's generation still refer to it as The Union. It and Dr Steeven's Hospital were landmarks in our community.

The area also had a laundry, Dunlop's, where my mother used to leave my dad's collars to be starched crisp. Despite the cost, seven collars were left every Saturday and collected every Tuesday. Guinness expected their staff to look well turned out. Fresh, clean, starched collars were a must.

Guinness was the major employer in the area and the best. The conditions were excellent. To get a job there was considered a great achievement in terms of securing your future. Working conditions in the brewery were far superior to many other places of employment. Guinness looked after its staff well. They had their own doctor, dentist and chemist. The whole family was looked after up to the time the children left school. Pensions were generous and Guinness was one of the first employers to provide a widow's pension.

I remember the streets as always being busy, with people walking to and from work. Bread men, milkmen, butchers, and delivery boys with their boxcars, delivered their wares. The rush hour, as we know it today, didn't exist. There were few cars on the road then, but there was a buzz that had a much nicer energy than when the area became more prosperous.

Our house was on the main road. We had no front garden. My Mam didn't like us playing in the front as the road was busy, but the back garden was quite big. In fact the garden appeared huge to us. Our friends and cousins often came to our house to play. In those days you could stay out there all day and feel you were miles away from home.

The garden was split into sections: a little patch where my mam had her flowers and grass, and then a wild part with bushes and trees and long grass. At the very end of the garden flowed the Camac River. It was a dirty, litter-filled river, which would flood our garden almost every winter, and the back of the house more than once.

In our garden was a swing, but not a posh swing. This was one we had made ourselves, with rope going from one tree to another. It was great and we could fly much higher than any of those shop-bought swings some of our neighbours had. The higher it went the better. An old wooden shed stood at the end of the garden. It was once a chicken shed where my older brother had kept chickens for a short time. When the chickens left my mother turned it into a playhouse for us, mainly for my sisters to play mammies and daddies in. She had put her sewing skills to use again and had transformed this old chicken hut into a playhouse where we spent long summer days playing to our hearts' content. Every other day Mam would bring us down biscuits and orange squash and they tasted so good.

The garden was our adventure playground. We spent hours there and our friends loved to come to play. It was like having a little piece of the country in the heart of Dublin.

Chapter 5

This was the wonderful place where the Angels came to me often, but only when I was in the garden on my own. In the early days they just stood close by and watched me play. They didn't speak. I was never afraid of them. Looking back, I know I firmly believed what Mam had told me about the Angels. They were sent to watch over you, so in my mind I thought they came to keep me safe when I was alone. They were always very gentle and never did anything to frighten me.

I enjoyed playing with my friends, but I was a bit of a loner as a child. I didn't seem to need other people around me. The Angels made everything feel safe and I never felt lonely. The Angels stood very tall and appeared in bright rainbow-like colours with big wings that you could almost see through. As the years went by, they became much more defined.

Perhaps I'm looking back with rose-tinted glasses, but they were great days. I did feel safe and happy there, without a thought of the outside world.

The house was always busy, with people coming and going and with different sounds and noises coming from each room. It was a bit of a madhouse at times, with my sisters playing music in one room, and the radio blasting out in another. All the while my older brothers would be watching sport on the television. But if this sounds a bit cosy, the Waltons we were not! We got on most of the time, but like most big families we had our disagreements. Then all hell would break loose.

My mother would soon put a stop to it all. She was quite firm and we did as we were told without question. Mam never hit us, but she would "punish" us, as she put it, by keeping us in from play or not letting us go somewhere with our friends. And she never backed down. She meant what she said, so we didn't argue or try to get her to change her mind. We all had our jobs to do around the house and garden and we just got on with it.

My mother's days were filled with cooking, cleaning and shopping. There were no supermarkets in my younger days, so we got the messages in the local shops. Bread, milk and vegetables in Smith's at the top of the hill. Meat was always bought in the butcher's and only from Bob Carroll facing St Kevin's Hospital. You got other bits and pieces in Conway's. You brought the slop from your mam's kitchen to Miss Conway's for the pig man. This was really worth doing because when you handed in the slop you got a free bar of toffee.

The other goodies came from Camac Stores. Every shop had something the others didn't have, and we always knew where to get what. On Sundays after roast-beef dinner, we had our dessert: ice-cream and jelly. We didn't have a fridge at that time, so every Sunday just before lunch we were sent out to get the ice-cream from the Camac Stores. It was shut on Sundays, but Miss Coady the owner lived over the shop with her brother. So we'd knock on this big green door, hoping she would answer. When we heard her unlocking the door we were relieved, knowing that there was a treat in store. Sometimes she was cross with us for knocking on Sundays, but more often than not she was glad of the business, I'm sure. Thank God for Miss Coady living so near. Raspberry ripple ice-cream with strawberry jelly to die for.

My favourite memories of my early days are the smell of Sunday dinner, of toast by the fire on winter nights and the smell and feel of fresh, clean, crisp white sheets. It still makes me feel warm and good inside to think of those happy times.

Chapter 6

Every summer I would leave the city to spend four to five weeks in Wexford on my grandmother's farm. My grandmother lived on a modest farm, in a small country house on about sixty acres of land. My uncle Tommy and Aunt Alice worked the farm. It was a typical farm of its time. They kept cows, pigs, a couple of horses and lots of chickens. Work started very early in the morning and finished late in the evening. My favourite job was going for the cows in the evening with Aunt Alice.

Alice was the kindest of souls and had the greatest respect for the land and her animals. She was so kind to them and always knew when they were sick. She had names for all the farm animals, even the chickens. She was also funny. She had two dogs and she called them both Sheila. I thought it was very strange and she would always give a big laugh when I asked her why. She was also a great woman for telling you ghost stories. She'd have the hair standing on the back of your neck and then you would have to get her to sleep with you that night, you were so scared.

Every evening, on our way to bring home the cows, she would remind me it was six o'clock. We would say the Angelus, reciting it very slowly and with great faith. Then the dogs gathered the cows together and walked them back to the farm. Alice would milk the cows before taking them back to the field. Then we would go in and have a large supper:

usually homemade bread, cold meat, or eggs and rashers and *always* homemade jam.

Sunday was the most important day of the week. On Sunday we'd get up and do only jobs that really needed to be done. Then we'd get washed and put on our best clothes. The day was kept very sacred and it was always quiet and peaceful. Even the animals were quiet. The energy of that day was very different to the rest of the week; it felt special. Everything slowed down and the world felt at rest. At 11 a.m. we all headed off to second Mass in the village church of Oilgate. It was in this very church that I first heard the word "healer", a word that has stayed with me for the rest of my life. I was about seven or eight at the time. As I came out of church holding on to my dad's hand, a man came up to us. He had a very friendly conversation with Dad and, just before he left, he turned to me, shook my hand, looked me in the eyes and winked. Then he turned to my dad and said, "You have a very powerful healer here, Aidan; you'd better look after him." They shook hands and the man left. I didn't know what he meant, nor did I question it. But it was something that stayed in my mind. I often thought of this encounter over the following years, wondering what he'd meant.

The year would start to close in again, and once November arrived it was time to start thinking about Christmas. The Christmas pudding was mixed around the end of November. I still recall the smell of the spices as it cooked on top of the stove. The kitchen was wet from steam because you had to boil puddings for eight hours. Then, and only then, when you got that pudding smell, could you look forward to the big day and hope you would get a wonderful Christmas present.

The Christmas tree was always put up around the 18th or 19th of December. It was decorated with every colour and shape of shiny decorations you could get your hands on. We kept our fingers crossed the fairy lights would work. So between the smells of plum pudding and the pine tree scenting the room, Christmas was my favourite time of the year.

I loved the whole story of Jesus and how He was born. This was the only time in the year that you heard the Angels mentioned. I was always very happy to hear about them.

After Mass on Christmas morning we came home, played with our presents and had fizzy lemonade and biscuits. Sometimes we paid a visit to our aunts and uncles, or maybe they would come to our house. Then once again it was time to ring out the old year on New Year's Eve, and ring in the new. And the cycle started all over again.

Chapter 7

I had looked forward to starting school. It was June and the feast of the Sacred Heart. On my way home from Mass with my mother, we passed Basin Lane Convent School. It was a big, grey, two-storey building with vast windows and a huge, green, double front door. High green railings lined the front of the building.

The school was not strange to me, as I had left my youngest sister to school many times with Mam over the past few years. We didn't enter through the main door; instead Mam led me around by the convent chapel and in through a side door. We went out through the small playground to another hall. She knocked on a big mahogany door, from behind which we could hear the sound of children doing their lessons.

As the door opened it creaked a little. From behind it appeared a very small figure of a woman dressed from head to toe in black. She wore rimless glasses and had pale skin and rosy cheeks. Her voice was kind and warm and she had a bright smile. As she looked at me she gently placed her hands on my head. She listened to my mother as she asked if it were possible to enrol me to start school in the coming September. The nun's name was Sister Imelda.

When my mother was finished, Sister Imelda looked down at me and asked, "Well, young man, what do you think? Would you like to come to school when the summer holidays are over?" Nodding my head in agreement and terrified at the same time, I finally got out the words: "Yes, please."

She smiled and said, "Well we had better put your name on the roll." She went back into the classroom, leaving the door half open. I could see all the boys had their heads in their arms on the desk as if they were asleep. Sister Imelda came back to us with the biggest book I had ever seen. When she opened it, it seemed there were hundreds of names written in it. She wrote my name, address and date of birth in the roll with a pen that she dipped in dark blue ink. Then she dried it off with clean white blotting paper.

"There you are," she said. "You're a big boy now. You be good for your mammy and I will see you in September." She smiled at my mother and shook her hand and then placed an oval-shaped red badge of the Sacred Heart in my hand. "Wear that and Holy God will mind you," she told me.

I was delighted with my badge and couldn't wait to start school. On our way home Mam did the shopping in Smith's and told me to pick out some biscuits for myself for being so good in front of the nun. As always, I pointed at the box of butter creams and said, "I'll have those, please."

That's all I remember until that September and my first day walking to school with my schoolbag on my back, holding my mother's hand. I was very excited and couldn't wait to get to the classroom. The hall was packed with mothers and children. It wasn't the quiet hall I remembered from my previous visit. Most of the children were crying and mothers were talking to each other, trying to be heard over the howling children.

Sister Imelda sat in her classroom marking the roll as the mothers dropped the children off. The noise and the crying terrified me. It dawned on me that I was going to be left here. Mam wasn't going to be staying. What would I do? I had never been on my own. The tears ran down my cheeks as Mam forced my hand out of hers.

She kissed me and told me everything would be fine. She said she would be outside in the hall waiting for me. My heart was racing as I saw her walk away and I really felt I would never see her again.

The room appeared to be huge. It was a big double room with four very large Victorian windows on each side and a gallery at the back. Long benches lined the room and boys sat everywhere. Some were crying, some just waited quietly, and a few played with other boys. At the top of the room behind the teacher's desk stood a beautiful white wooden altar with a statue of Our Lady and one of the Sacred Heart. Red lights glowed in front of them. Fresh flowers in big glass vases stood on either side of the altar. The walls where covered with drawings of nursery rhymes, and pictures of all the saints and holy people you could think of.

One picture that stood out from the rest was one of a beautiful Angel flying across the sky holding children's hands, bringing them safely to the other side of a valley. My mother was right again. My Angels were here and they would keep me safe in school. "They never leave your side," she told me again and again.

I can't remember what we did for the rest of the day, but I do remember seeing my mam at the gate when we came out. I can still feel the joy and happiness I felt when I hugged her. I hoped I would never have to go back to school or leave her again. It came as something of a shock to go back the next day!

Everything soon settled and school became part of my daily life. I went without much fuss and loved Sister Imelda. She was a loving teacher and I don't recall her shouting or being cross with us. My best ever day was the day she said she was going to teach us the Guardian Angel prayer. I was so excited because I knew it and for some reason she knew I knew it. She asked me if

I would like to recite it for the class. When I finished she patted me gently on my head and told me I was a great boy and very special. "Your Angels are with you," she said. I took it that she could see them as they were everywhere in the room. She gave me a picture of Our Lady of Knock as a reward for saying the prayer.

The next day she told us about our Angels and about Jesus and His Mother. The room filled with Angels when she spoke of them and one stood beside every boy in the room. No one said anything, so I assumed that everybody else could see them. They had become a little clearer for me by now. They stood about six foot high and were as bright as the night stars.

Their wings, attached to their backs, stood firm and straight. I was not afraid of these beautiful Beings of Light. They always brought with them an energy of calm and safety, and I never questioned anything I saw. These were the Angels my mother and

Sister Imelda spoke about so they *had* to be real. Nuns and mothers never lied.

I spent three very happy years in Basin Lane School and had three extremely nice teachers. Sister Imelda prepared us for our big day, our First Holy Communion. Every afternoon she taught us the prayers we needed for our First Confession and First Communion. She had no Communion wafers, so we practised with the flat medal that hung from her rosary beads. She would say "Corpus Christi". We would answer "Amen" and then she would place the medal on our tongue, take it away and pass to the next boy, and so on. She also prepared us for our First Confession.

I was not looking forward to that. We all walked down to the church the Friday morning before our Communion day. Two in a row, hand in hand. We waited our turn to go into the confession box. It was terrible; a dark and lonely place that smelled musty.

As I stood there terrified and shaking, hoping I wouldn't forget my sins, a noise came from behind the grid. The priest pulled open the little flap and muttered something. I can still remember his old, grim, pasty face. He looked away into space, not really listening to me at all. I'm sure he was bored, as we all had the same sins to confess.

When I was finished he muttered something about being "a good boy for your mammy and teachers". Then he added, "And don't hurt God by being bold again." He told me to say "three Hail Marys for your penance", made the sign of the cross and closed the flap. I was in the dark again.

From now on you had to be good or God would be very cross with us if you. If you told lies or said bad words, this would hurt God and you would nail Him to the cross all over again. What a big responsibility this was for a six-year-old.

I woke up early on the morning of my First Communion feeling very excited. Everyone got up to get me ready and to see me off to the church. I wore a Glen check grey suit with short trousers, white shirt and a blue tie. Mam dressed me and she told me how handsome I was. My brothers and sisters all teased me and said how all the girls would run after me. When I was ready, my dad and mam took me to the church. Dad drove us and I was allowed to sit in the front seat.

The church was full. All the girls in their white dresses and veils sat on one side, the boys in their suits of different colours on the other. The mothers and fathers sat behind us. There was a great feeling of happiness in the air.

When I received Holy Communion for the first time, it felt nothing like Sister Imelda's medal, and it didn't taste like it either. It tasted just like wafer and you had to be careful not to let it stick to the roof of your mouth. If it did you were not under *any* circumstance allowed to put your finger into your mouth. That would be a most dreadful sin and you might even be struck *dead* because only the priest could touch the Body of Christ. Only he was pure enough. All you could do was try and take it away, using your tongue to peel it off the roof of your mouth, and hope that in the process you didn't swallow your tongue. You could never chew the host either: it must *never* touch your teeth.

Thank God none of these much-dreaded things happened on the day, so I was safe. I hadn't committed any sin and the Body and Blood of Christ would make me strong and good.

After my Communion I had one more happy year in Basin Lane in first class. Then, in June of that year, just before we broke up for summer holidays, we went into what was called the big boys' school. This school was run by the Christian Brothers. It was only across the road, but what a difference crossing the road would make in my life.

Chapter 8

These where not to be my happiest days. In fact they were days of hell, but I didn't have any choice and had to go. From the first time I entered that school I became very nervous and insecure. I had a couple of very nice teachers, but I was not happy.

They "streamed" the classes and I was put into the top stream. This meant I was separated from most of my friends. I was placed into a class with new boys I didn't know and I had to make friends all over again.

I was always quite shy and it wasn't easy for me to make friends. However, as time passed and I started to make friends, I didn't mind so much and settled down to the routine of school. The following year, things started to get better. I had made it into the A-grade stream and my mother and father were very proud of me. The year started, as always, getting new books and getting used to a new teacher.

The master we had this particular year was an elderly gentleman – very refined, immaculately dressed, rather dapper and with grey hair. He wore a signet ring on his left hand. During the time I was in his class I started to develop a bad pain in my right-hand side that made me very pale and left me feeling sick. When this happened the teacher was always very kind. He'd put his chair by the heater for me and, after he'd had his break, he would bring me back a mug of hot milk and pepper. He'd tell me to drink it slowly. When it was time to go home he'd always make sure one of the boys that lived near me would walk home with me.

As very nervous child, I worried if I didn't understand something or if I couldn't do my homework. In fact, I worried so much about reading aloud in class that my mother spoke to the teacher and told him how upset I was. He reassured her that she should not concern herself. He said that he would have a word with me during the day.

Words he did have with me – and a lot more besides. At the tender age of nine, this teacher, whom my mother and I trusted implicitly, and whom we thought of as a gentleman, sexually abused me regularly for a year.

It started with him asking me to stay behind after school. He wanted to have a word with me, he said. My mother had told him I was worried about my lessons. When all the other boys had left he went over to the door, locked it and put the keys in his pocket. Then, very slowly, he walked from window to window closing the Venetian blinds until the room was in twilight. He bent down and told me how special I was and how I was his pet and that I needn't worry about anything. And then he began his abuse of me.

I didn't know what he was doing then. I knew it wasn't right, but how could I explain this to anybody? I didn't know what was happening. We were always told to respect our teacher and never to give back cheek and always do as we were told. So this was what I did, but from that first day of shock and horror, I hated going to school even more.

I stopped going out to play when I got home and I didn't mix or even play much with my classmates. I was so afraid and nervous that I had to get my mother to walk me to school every morning. I hoped and prayed every day that this man would leave me alone. As the abuse became more regular my Angels became stronger and came to my rescue when it happened. It was happening once or twice a week and I always dreaded the last bell ringing. To this day a shiver runs up and down my body when I hear the lock click on a door or the noise of Venetian blinds closing.

I remember praying one day as he was closing the blinds, with the tears running down my face, and my body shaking like a leaf, *Please, my Guardian Angel, help me.* As I stood there, a beautiful figure of a very tall Angel came to me. He was dressed in pink and green shimmering robes, with pure white skin and piercing pale blue eyes.

"Don't worry," he said. "Take my hand," and as I did I had the strangest of feelings. I felt my body moving away from where I was standing and I began to float. The Angel took me over to the door, and sat me on top of the press. I could see myself standing over at the blackboard with the teacher, but could feel nothing. The Angel stood beside me and then unfolded his wings and placed them around me. I felt somehow safe and he whispered gently, "You are safe, it will be OK." This, I think, was the first time I heard an Angel speak, but the voice didn't seem to penetrate or even enter the space of the room. I still can't explain it, but Angels seem to speak outside of our space and energy and their voices fall softly and gently.

This was a very strange experience: I now know that it was an out-of-body-experience. I saw myself in the room and I felt myself on top of the press, but for the first time I couldn't feel what this man was doing to me. The Angel had eased the pain of it all. I was scared and very confused, but the Angel said repeatedly, "You are safe, you are not feeling anything."

When the teacher had finished abusing me, the Angel took my hand and led me back to where I was standing. My two bodies merged and I was one again, numb with shock and unable to utter a word.

I always felt dirty and somehow guilty after the abuse. I would rush out to the toilets to wash my hands, my mouth and my face before the short journey home, which seemed to take forever. Everyone else from my class was at home by now and the lane was empty and silent. For me this was good. At least no one could see my shame. My Angels were the only ones with me, but even they were silent.

That day an Angel had spoken to me for the first time and on the way home they spoke again. Every few minutes they placed their hands on my shoulders and whispered, "Everything will pass, Little Soul, and you will feel good again." I always did when I got home and my mother gave me a big hug and I could breathe and feel safe again. And on those days I always held on to my mam for a little longer. Once I was at home I was safe and nothing could harm me. Then I'd have my dinner and Mam would sit with me and help me with my homework before the rest of the family came home from school and work.

Looking back I see how supportive she was, but I didn't have the language to express myself and tell her what was happening to me.

Morning came quickly on those days, and the dread and the fear built up again. I would hope against hope that I could leave my classroom safely, when school was over, and go home with the rest of my classmates. But as the year went on the abuse continued and I became more and more of a loner. I never wanted to go out and I only felt safe when my mother or one of my family was with me.

During the next few months the Angels were with me all the time, but their presence became stronger every time that teacher locked the door. They came and took me out of my body and took me to the press. They instructed me to place my hands over my eyes. "Let's have fun and let's fly and see all the beautiful things in the world." They took me where children are safe and they talked to me a little more, but as a child, because that is what I was. At no time did they say anything I didn't understand. They knew how upset I was, so they showed me places and took me flying high in the sky, holding me very tightly and showing me the beautiful colours of nature, the seas, the forests, the meadows and the snow-capped mountains. They showed me glorious places, pointing out the different colours and the beauty of, as they called it, "God's work". It looked just like the picture of the Angel and the children in Sister Imelda's room. They also took me to what they called "The Garden of the Angels". What a beautiful place it was. In a huge flower garden the Angels gathered the essences from the flowers to take to earth, to bring healing and love. Flowers of every shape and colour grew everywhere. It was a place of peace, full of trees, lakes and waterfalls.

A pearly white mist covered the entire area. Their feet didn't seem to touch the grass beneath them as they moved with gentleness and ease from place to place, not bumping into each other. They were not singing as I'd thought they would be; there was stillness and silence instead. My Angel, whom I was calling Aidan, told me this was where the Angels gathered and waited for the people on earth to call them and ask them for help and guidance. They dressed in different colours, in simple, long, flowing robes. They were all about the same height. Their hair was of different colours too, and they had pale skin with powder pink cheeks. All of them smiled and they had the most beautiful bright piercing blue eyes. My Angels told me to remember this place and to remember to ask them for their help. How could I forget this place? It was beautiful. Words or pictures could never do it justice.

"It's time for you to go back. Everything is okay now and this will pass, Little Soul. You are very special and very strong. Don't be afraid, we will help you." Very gently they took me back to that classroom and to my place of fear and terror. Once more I rushed out of the classroom and ran home as quick as I could to feel safe and loved again.

I never told anyone about the abuse or about the Angels. It wasn't that I didn't want to; it was that I didn't know how to. The year finally came to an end and we moved to a new classroom and a new teacher. He was a nice man, and a very good teacher, but I didn't trust him either. I knuckled down, worked hard, faded as much into the background as I could, and did as I was told. Doing as I was told came easy to me. This class was good for me and I enjoyed school a little more again. I tried to put the horrible experience of the previous year out of my head.

This peace that came into my life was to be short-lived when I passed from this class into a Christian Brother's class. He was a small man with a reputation of being hard and very nasty. He had a red, scurvy face, black hair, shining with Brylcreem, combed to the side. He had cold, empty, mean, brown squinty eyes that stared at you from behind black-rimmed glasses. He stank of nicotine and mothballs and his shoulders where covered in thick, white dandruff.

Believe me, there was nothing Christian about this man and he should never have been allowed to teach, or to be in a room with such young souls. He practised a different type of abuse – not sexual abuse, but an abuse that was just as horrendous and just as soul-destroying. It was a mental, degrading, physical abuse that robbed me of my spirit – the real me – and put in its place an empty, lost and fearful child. At the age of eleven I didn't know who I was any more and felt worthless and a complete failure. This is how this man of God taught me and most of my classmates to think of ourselves. I wasn't the only one in the class he did this to; there were others, but I was the one he did it to most often.

This Christian Brother didn't like me from day one. His first few words to the class were that we were there to learn and learn we would, and if we were slow and stupid, well then we would have to work harder or we would be left behind. "Because I don't work with stupid boys," he sneered.

Then he used a term that I will never forget. He said there were two types of boys: the bright boys who were intelligent – and these were the boys he preferred to have in his class – and the "dumbcluckers". These were the people that would never amount to anything. Everyone laughed, including myself. He then went on to explain that he had all our books in his room for the coming year. He told us the only one missing was the religion book. As we had a religion test at the end of September every year, he didn't know what we were going to do.

I put up my hand and tried to explain to him that this had happened last year too. We had just worked from the religion book we had the previous year. He gave me a look, then said, "Now that's what I mean. Every year I get at least one, and here he is… your dumbclucker! Sit down you stupid, stupid boy and don't let me hear you talk again until you can make sense." He turned to the class, shook his head and smiled, giving them permission to laugh, and so they did. About an hour later the Brother from next door came in and asked him the same question about the religion book. He wondered what they should do for the exam at the end of the month. "Well Storey?" our teacher shouted at the top of his voice. "Stand up."

Turning to the other Brother, he said, "Storey here will explain all about what you have to do as he knows everything." So again I tried to explain what happened the previous year. Halfway through he told me to shut up and sit down. Turning back to his colleague, he said, "This is my dumbclucker for this year, God help me." Again they all laughed and the two Christian Brothers shook their heads. I felt sick and totally humiliated. I just wanted to cry and run home, but I couldn't. I saw my Angel very clearly in the classroom again and I knew there were going to be difficult times ahead. The Angel put his finger to his lips as if to tell me not to say a word.

On the way home I was on my own. I was very ashamed and didn't want to be with anybody, afraid they would jeer at me. That would make me very upset and I didn't want to let them see that.

On that day, as on many other days, my Angels walked beside me and assured me that everything would be all right and that later I would see clearly why this was happening to me. As we walked they told me all I had to do was ask for their help and they would be there, and to remember that they were *always* with me. I didn't understand their words until many years later.

I put up with the same insults week after week. I had decided I wasn't going to the CB secondary school. I had had enough of the Brothers, so I didn't do the entrance exam, much to this teacher's annoyance. I had decided, with my parents' consent, to go to the local Vocational School in Inchicore.

By the last two months of my stay in that school, I was counting the days. The Brother decided to give us a summer test. He loved giving tests. As we were about to finish our maths test I tapped the boy in front of me to ask him for my rubber, which he had borrowed earlier, as I needed to correct something. When the exam was over the boy sitting beside me asked the boys behind me if they had seen what I had done. The two boys behind me said, "Yes, he was copying." I couldn't believe it when my so-called friend, whom I had known for years, went up to the Brother and told him I was copying from the boy in front of me. I didn't know what to do.

He looked at me with his eyes popping, his face as red as a tomato and the blood vessels in his neck about to burst. He shouted at the top of his voice.

"Storey, come up here, you cheat." He stood me in front of the class and told me that I was stupid, a cheat, and a good-for-nothing fool. I stood there and I started to cry. "Look at you," he shouted. "Crying and shivering like all cowards when caught doing no good. Look at the state of you." Then he spoke the words I will never forget. He asked, "What are you, a man or a mouse?" He waited a few seconds for me to answer but I couldn't; all I could do was cry. His next words were to haunt me for twenty years: "You are nothing," he said. "Do you hear me? *Nothing.* And do you know what, Storey? You will never amount to *anything.* Get back to your desk, you good-for-nothing waster."

That was my last day in that school. When I got home and told my mother she told me to stop worrying, that I wasn't going back and she would deal with it from here. The next day she went to the school. When he came to the door to speak to my mother, he told her he didn't want me back in his class. To his shock my mother told him she had no intention of ever letting me near him again. She said that he wasn't fit to wear the collar of God and that some day he would have to pay for what he had done to a child. He told her that she could get into trouble with the school authorities if she were to keep me at home for the next six weeks.

At this she looked him in the eyes and said, "Well then, my dear man, you will have a lot of explaining to do. My son may be nothing to you, but he is the world to me. I love him and I have seen you take every piece of his childhood from him, but enough is enough. No more from today."

Many years later my mother was at a fundraising event in the parish and this Brother happened to be there. On the way out, the woman she was with turned to say hello to him and my mother stood with her. When they were finished speaking, Mam introduced herself to him. "I'm Mrs Storey. Do you remember me?"

"No," he said.

"Well, well," said my mother. "You should. I had to knock on your door often enough. I'm Aidan Storey's mother: do you not remember him? He remembers you."

"Oh, yes," he replied. "I do now. How is he doing?"

Do you know what she said to this tormentor of children? My lovely mother said, "He is doing very well, no thanks to you, and despite all you put him through. I hope God can find it in his heart to forgive you when your time comes." Then she said to him, "You know people say about the Christian Brothers, give them your boy and they will give you back a man. I gave you my boy and you gave me back a broken boy and, do you know what? Despite all you put him through, he is more of a man than you will ever be." She was so proud that night when she got home as she sat and told me what she had done.

Chapter 9

Life stared to improve again when I left primary school. I spent that summer in Dublin. I got a dog around this time. Her name was Trixie, a crossbreed black, curly dog who stole my heart from the moment she arrived in the house.

They say that pets come into your life when you most need them, and boy did I need her. She showered me with love and protection from the moment she entered my life. She took my mind off the past years and stopped me worrying about starting my new school in September. I took her for walks every day and this also gave me time alone with the Angels.

The Angels were still gentle with me and walked by my side, just talking about general things, like how I was doing. Every now and then they would reassure me that everything would be fine in my new school and that I would do well. I really wanted to believe this. It was at this time that I asked them about other people's Angels. I told them that I could see Angels around people often, but not all the time, and that when I was younger I saw them everywhere. They explained I could still do this, but because I was so upset in school for the past few years I had blocked it out. I wasn't able to concentrate, but in time I would see them again. Then, one day in St Stephen's Green in the city centre, after walking the dog, I sat down to enjoy the sun and to rest before I started my journey home.

It was a lovely late August day and although the park was busy I had managed to find a quiet spot to let the dog off her lead. I sat looking at the people, who seemed almost far away. There was a strange but very comforting silence and peace hung over my space. Then the Angels made themselves visible to me. They were laughing and sat on either side of me. My Angel spoke and again the sound of his voice didn't seem to enter the space I was in. The gentle sound just flowed into my hearing. "Would you like to see the Angels at work?" he asked.

"Yes, please," I said, not knowing what he meant. But I felt safe and by this time Trixie had come and sat beside me. I am sure she could see them. The Angels told me to look across the park where lots of people were, some sitting, some lying down, some walking. Then I was instructed to close my eyes and open them again. When I looked back at the people there was a sea of Angels with them. Their robes were different colours and they were standing by the people to whom they were assigned. Everyone had at least two Angels and they all looked happy. "What are they doing?" I asked.

"They are protecting them and helping them just as we do you."

"That's good. That one over there," I said, pointing at a middle-aged woman sitting on a park bench. "What is the Angel doing with her?" I asked.

"This woman is feeling a little sick. She has a bad headache and her Angels are healing her by placing their hands on her head."

"Really? So that's what you do to heal someone, is it?" I said, remembering the word "healer" that the man had used about me in Wexford when I was a young child.

"Well, it's not quite that simple. We will show you how it's done another day," they said, and smiled at each other. Over by the pond a number of Angels walked or stood at the edge, almost in the water.

"What are they doing in the water?" I asked.

"You see the children playing? They are keeping them safe and protecting them from falling into the pond," they explained. It looked as if the Angels where playing with the children. They ran in and out and all around them, helping them to catch their ball. They cushioned their falls and made them gentle so the children wouldn't hurt themselves. Their robes flowed like a silk rainbow in the summer breeze. They walked very close to the old people and it was as if they held their arms and gently guided them along their way.

"This is what we do. We help people and we make it safe for them. We show you this so you won't worry about anything and to let you know we are here for you. Ask us for anything and we will give it to you as long as it is for your higher good."

I wasn't quite sure what was meant by "higher good".

"I just want to be happy in school next month and to like my teachers," I said.

"We promise you this will happen and we also want you to enjoy yourself and have fun again. We love you very much and we are your friends."

I made my way home and a great feeling of peace came over me that day. I didn't fear the start of school after that. I started school in Inchicore a couple of weeks later and loved it. The teachers were people who really cared about you and helped if you didn't understand something. I couldn't believe it. This was the way school should be.

Very slowly I began to trust teachers again. Shortly after I started, my mother was called to the school. They were concerned about the number of days I had missed the previous year in primary. When Mam told the principal my story, she was assured that nothing like the bullying by that Christian Brother would ever happen in this school and that he would inform all my teachers of what had happened to me. From that day on, to the day of my Leaving Certificate, the teachers were wonderful to me. School was good again, although I never really had the confidence I would have liked to have.

Chapter 10

I was still having visits from my Angels and I started to relax with them quite a lot. They spoke to me about the importance of having fun and not letting the past hold me back. They shimmered in their beautiful pale robes. Every day over the years these beautiful Beings of Light would come visit me and help me with anything that was worrying me.

Then, one day in school, when I was about fourteen, my classmates started talking about ghosts, spirits and the devil. And about what they did, and about haunted houses and how spirits could overtake you and make you do things that were evil. I heard myself asking the question out loud. "What about your Guardian Angels? Don't they keep you safe from all that evil stuff?"

My friends all looked at me and laughed. "You are joking, aren't you? Sure, nobody believes in that, you eejit." I laughed back at them as if to say, *only joking.*

This played on my mind for the rest of the day and evening. The next day was Saturday and after breakfast I went down to the end of our garden beside the river and called on my Angels to come. Within seconds they were there standing in front of me. A beautiful white mist engulfed us. They looked more serene than ever that morning. The Angel I called Aidan spoke to me: "Good morning, Little Soul. You are worried and a bit nervous today. Look – your energy is all flat. Tell me, what can I do for you?"

I turned to them. "You are Angels, is that right?"

"Yes we are."

"Can everyone see you or is it just me?"

"Oh, my blessed child, everyone can see us but most choose not to."

"Why can I? Why me?"

"Because you ask us for our help and you always knew of our existence."

"What do you do and where do you come from?"

"We come from the same place you come from: God. The same God that made you made us. He made us to help and look after you in life. We are your friends."

"So I don't need to be afraid of you?"

"Never. We are here to protect you."

"Why can I see you and what do you want from me?" I asked.

"You see because you believe, and you never questioned. And you are here to help others to see and work with us. The people have forgotten about us and don't work with us anymore."

"So, what do you want me to do?"

"You will tell people about us and our great power and how we can help them and make their lives easier. You too will also help people and healing will come through you."

I panicked. I didn't understand this. I was sure I wouldn't be able to do it. And there it was again, that word... *healing*.

"I can't do this. Nobody will listen to me. No, no," I protested. He looked at me and smiled and then he spoke very gently.

"Not now. But in time you will do this work and we will teach you more." They enfolded me; their wings surrounded me in a group-like hug, before they left.

That weekend, loneliness engulfed me. I didn't know what was going on. Was this all in my head? Were they really there? But then, I thought, they are they to help me. Weren't they always around? Didn't my mother and Sister Imelda speak about them? Aren't they always mentioned in Mass? On and on I argued with myself.

I just didn't know what to think. My head was bursting so I decided to ask a couple of people I really trusted. First I would ask my mam. As she worked her way around the kitchen, I started with my questions. "Mam, you know your Guardian Angel? Well, is he with you all the time?"

"Oh, he is," she said firmly. "Even when you sleep; they never leave your side."

Good, I thought. At least they are there and Mam believes in them. Now for the big one: "Do you talk to yours, Mam?"

"Oh, I do, son. I'm always talking to her. She always helps and keeps me out of danger," Mam assured me.

"That's great," I said. "Do you ever see your Angel and sit and talk with her?"

"Oh no, son; nobody can see them. They are only spirits and you can't see spirits, but you just know they are there."

"Right," I said. "You don't see them.

They are spirits… but can some people see them?"

"Well, some very holy people and some saints have seen them, but not everyone. But don't be worrying about that, Aidan love. You don't need to see them. You just need to know that they are there."

I decided to leave it at that. Angel, spirit or ghost – which one was it? I fretted.

I then asked a good friend, whose opinion I respected, on my way home from school one day. "Do you believe in Angels?" I was hoping against hope his answer would be "yes".

"No way!" he said emphatically. "That's mad stuff. Superstition. Someone hanging out of you with wings and keeping you from danger?" he scoffed. "Yeah, well where are they when someone is murdered or killed in a car crash? No, it's a load of crap," he said confidently.

"Okay," I persisted. "What about ghosts?"

"Yeah I *definitely* believe in ghosts. Everyone knows someone who has seen them, so they are there and most of them are evil."

I was shocked. "What do you mean, *evil?*" I demanded.

"Well they do terrible things on earth and their spirit lives on forever and they get no rest. This is their punishment. Sometimes they even pretend to be good spirits and say they will help you. Then they take your soul and you are left wandering the earth forever," he declared.

I had heard enough from him. I decided not to ask any more. He was frightening the life out of me. I would give it one more try, I decided. I would run it by another friend and see what she had to say. She was in the Legion of Mary with me and I only met her on Wednesday nights. We were chatting away and I asked her about ghosts or spirits and if she believed in them.

"Yes, I most certainly do – without question," she said. "They are people who died before their time and their spirit roams the earth until their time is up and then God calls them to rest."

"Right," I said. "So they are not evil and they wouldn't do you any harm?" I asked, longing for reassurance.

"Well, I am not sure about that. I wouldn't want to be a room on my own with one," she said, and she laughed.

"Okay then, what do you think about Angels? Do we all have one?" I persisted.

"I don't think so," she said, much to my dismay. "We were told this as children so we wouldn't be afraid. Sure, we don't need them. God will protect you," she added, with a great air of authority.

It was all very strange. People my own age didn't seem to believe in them, and as for seeing them… well, the Angels had said not everyone sees them.

My friends didn't believe they even existed. The guys in school thought I was an idiot. Even Mam didn't believe you could see them. According to her, only very holy people could see them, and that certainly wasn't me.

Maybe they were ghosts, I worried. Oh God, have I been talking to ghosts or was it all in my mind? I was plagued with doubts and fears.

That night I walked home alone after saying goodbye to my friend. The nerves got the better of me and I begged the Angels, or whatever they were, to please not come to me that night. When I got home I went to bed and I was so afraid that I slept with my head under the blankets for most of the night. Was I mad? What was going on? From that day on I was terrified of them and didn't want to be on my own.

A few days later it was a cold, wet day. I had come home from school and the house was empty. This was unusual as Mam was always there. I had sat down to do some homework when the Angels came and stood in front of me. My heart started to race. When I looked at them they looked more radiant than ever. Their energy was very soft and calm.

"Hello, Little Soul. Why are you so nervous and why does your heart beat so fast? Are you not happy to see us?" they asked gently.

What was wrong with me? I was never afraid of them and they always gave me such peace. Now I was so afraid I just wanted them to go. I found it difficult to speak.

"Yes, I am. No, I'm not. Oh leave me alone. You scare me," I heard myself say.

"Why are you afraid of us? We will not harm you. We are here to protect and mind you. Have we ever harmed you or hurt you, Little Soul?"

"No, but I don't want you to be around me anymore. Please stop coming to me. I'm not sure who you are and none of my friends believe you exist," I tried to explain.

"But you believe, don't you? That's why you see us. We have told you this many times. This is what makes you different and special."

"Well, I don't want to be different or special. I just want to be left alone and not be frightened. I want to be like everyone else." I heard myself say these words but at the same time I felt as if I was letting down a friend. They looked at me with their beautiful pale blue eyes and I could see love and understanding shine from them. One of them began to speak:

"We will give you what you want, Little Soul, and we will stop coming and stop being visible to you. But remember, we will never leave your side; we can't. As we explained before, we are with you forever. If you ever need us, just ask and we will come. Don't be afraid and remember there is no evil, only love. I know now that we will work together again. And I know you will talk about us again and again in the future. You will believe again. As we have told you time and time again, ask us for what you want and we will help you. So today, Little Soul, we will give you what you want. We will leave your sight but not your side. Don't be afraid. Go and search for what it is you need to learn and be joyous in your life."

Then, with a very gentle bow and a warm smile, they faded away very slowly into the white mist. The room became still and silent. I felt cold and alone, something I hadn't felt in a long, long time. I sat at the table, feeling very confused. These Angels were my friends. They had helped me and I always felt safe with them – but on the other hand maybe they were ghosts and that wouldn't be a good thing, I reasoned.

Chapter 11

From that day on I believed they were ghosts and didn't call on them again. I was spooked by them and didn't like being on my own any more. I even slept with my rosary beads in my hands every night, just in case they were evil and made an appearance.

I pretty much got on with my life. I finished school and went on to complete a business course. I found employment in Dublin with a small engineering firm. I worked in the administration department. Getting a job was a miracle in itself: it was the late 1970s, and work was almost impossible to find. It was a time when many young people were emigrating to all parts of the world and everything seemed bleak and grey.

It was a good place to work, but even then I just knew it wasn't what I should be doing. What I should be doing, I really didn't know. From time to time I still prayed to my Guardian Angel. I asked him to watch over me and guide me, but always with caution, as I still didn't want to see anything. I was in my late teens at this time and didn't want to go to pubs or nightclubs. They always left me feeling disconnected, tired and drained for the day.

I grew fearful and didn't know what was wrong with me. I became isolated from people and only wanted to be at home. My world was small but safe. To the outside world I am sure I looked like everyone else my age, but inside I was a lonely, sad individual who was very afraid of change. I was terrified at the thought of having a relationship. So I turned to God and the Church for help and guidance. I threw myself into it fully. No taking it easy with me!

Every evening on my way home from work I went to Mass. I started reading the Bible. I said the Rosary every night before I went to sleep. The Church became a sanctuary; it was good for me at that time. I read, and I asked questions, even though I believed everything the Church taught. And like most people now and in past generations, I focused on sin and on God's punishment, not on the love and compassion of God.

Now I had placed myself yet again in a place of control. I was very much controlled by everything I read or was taught by the Church. My mind became a hell to me yet again. For a short time everything I did, or even thought, I questioned. My past came back to haunt me. The hatred I had for the Christian Brother and the guilt I found in myself because I couldn't forgive him tormented me. That made me even worse than him in the eyes of God, as I saw it then. The memories of the sexual abuse plagued me. I tried hard over this period to put it out of my mind. I tried to convince myself that it had never happened; it was all in my mind. No, it wasn't abuse and, if it was, well then I had allowed it to happen. So that made me just as bad as that vile teacher, and how could I tell anyone about it?

I felt so dirty and unworthy of God's love. I went to confession time and time again, but just couldn't bring myself to say the words. I was now in my mid-twenties and still carried the pain, the guilt, and the shame. I continued going to church and looking for answers, but just couldn't find peace. Finally, in my late twenties, I fell into a deep depression and couldn't cope anymore. Everything had become too much.

Years passed and my depression deepened. In the late 1980s the sexual abuse stories had started to appear in the newspapers and on television. The stories had shocked the country and, like everyone, I was very upset. The difference was that the upset ran deep within me. The stories triggered the painful memories I had been trying to suppress. I was hurt and angry all over again.

This anger wasn't only about the children I was reading about; it was also about me. Deep inside, I was screaming. The sexual abuse was something I didn't want to admit to. I was afraid to think about it, afraid to bring up all the horrific feelings of pain and shame again. There it was – in their stories, and that word again… *special*.

Eventually it all fell into place. I was reading about myself in most of these reports and I was only one of the thousands who had gone through this nightmare. But what could I do? Should I tell someone? And if I did, would anyone believe me? If this really did happen, would people question why I'd keep it a secret for so long? After all, I was now in my mid-thirties. Did I really put it out of my head for all those years? Perhaps I could do it again: let sleeping dogs lie, I thought. He didn't rape me. I was overreacting. Let it go.

The more I tried, the more difficult it became to blot it out of my mind. I remembered every detail. The noise, the smells, the fear. My hands would start to sweat and my heart would race. My whole body was shaking. I'd feel dirty and unclean all over again. I needed to get rid of these feelings. I'd run into the shower and wash my body over and over again. Even after all these years, I still felt unclean – just as I had as a small boy.

And the questions remained unanswered:

Where do I go from here?

Who will help me?

Should I tell the family or my friends?

Then one evening on a walk, I ended up in the centre of town, in a church, waiting for confession. I was looking for answers and some direction. I thought maybe God would give me what I was looking for here in this church. Who better could you ask? Surely a priest could advise me on where to go or what to do.

When my turn came I went into the confession box. I knelt and waited for the priest to pull open the grid. When he did, a middle-aged priest with very little hair and a chubby face appeared.

I began, "Bless me, Father," and so on. Then I looked at him and decided I would tell him about what had happened and ask him what I should do. In a shaky voice I heard myself say, "Father, I was abused in school by a teacher when I was eight or nine."

"Abused?" He said, squinting. "What do you mean?"

"Sexually abused," I said.

"Sexually? Yes I see. So can you tell me about this so-called sexual abuse then?"

I was taken aback by his lack of compassion and concern, but I gave him the whole story and he listened with what I felt was great unease. When I was finished he didn't look at me. Instead he kept his eyes focused ahead of him and said, "You must examine your conscience and ask what part you played in this and why you left it so long to ask for God's forgiveness."

I was deeply shocked and said, "I didn't play any part, Father: do you understand? I'm looking for help. I was a child and, yes, it happened long ago. I need yours and God's help at this moment." I was almost pleading.

"You knew at the time that it was wrong, but you continued to allow it to take place – and you never thought of telling an adult about this? So did you not allow it to happen then? Go, young man, and examine your conscience." He shook his head in disgust and still didn't turn to look at me. He gave me absolution and my penance, shut the grid and left me in darkness.

I was deeply distressed. I couldn't believe it. It had taken me almost thirty years to speak to anyone about this. Or even to admit to myself that it had happened, and here I was, in a dark, musty box in the house of God, all alone.

I had moved beyond anger at this point. Numbness filled my body and mind. It took all my energy to get on my feet to push the door open. This numbness then seemed to explode and my entire body was filled with hatred. I spoke not a word as I made my way to the centre of the church to sit and reflect. From deep down inside my silence and in the quiet of the church, I felt the need to scream and shout and roar. How dare this man say what he had just said. With each step I took, the rage inside me expanded to proportions that words cannot even begin to describe.

I sat in the church and looked at my crucifix. Jesus – this Jesus I loved and who I knew loved me – where was He? I just couldn't get my head around any of this. Until now I had known at some level that I, the child, had no blame in that vile act. Now, this priest had planted a seed of doubt in my head.

I remember quite clearly that my arms and legs began to go numb, and that there was a deep ringing sound in my ears that echoed those words: "What part did you play?" Over and over it tormented me. I sat in numbness, unable to move, for what seemed an hour, wondering if I was in some way to blame.

The church was beginning to empty and the candles began to flicker in the dusky light. I looked at Jesus and said to Him, "I am tired, Jesus, just tired, and I don't understand what You or God want from me. At this moment I am *so* angry with you both. I came here looking for help – please don't break me again. Send me help and guidance because I can't do it anymore. I am tired of the battles."

As I was leaving I turned and said, "You know what? I'm not sure I can or want to do this anymore. I always try to do what is good and what is fair, but this is not what I get back. Give me a break, God. For once give me a break! As for you Angels saying, 'All you have to do is ask and we will give it to you…' Yeah, right! I'm fed up with you lot too. I'm tired of being on your side and getting nothing back. And you know what? I'm not sure about any of your airy-fairy stuff anymore. I'm totally exhausted and disgusted. Oh, and, by the way, I will never be back to confession again."

That night I went home numb and deflated and went to bed. As I lay in bed, I reflected on what had happened. I remembered how the Angels had helped me in the past. I remembered how they had come to my rescue and made things easier for me. I asked my Angels to help me that night, to bring me understanding and to help me find my God – the God of love and compassion. I was grateful that this episode hadn't happened a few years ago when I was in my depression. That would have really pushed me over the edge.

I finally drifted off to sleep. Later that night I awoke. The room was filled with a radiant white light. Within this brilliant white were orbs of different colours, mainly purple, green and gold. I reached out to touch the light, but could only feel its coolness and gentleness. The room felt safe and I was protected. I wasn't afraid, so I asked, "Who is there? Who are you and what do you want?"

From out of the silence a voice came: "It is us, Little Soul; we are here to help you. Do you want us to enter your space?"

My heart lifted.

"Yes, please. Please let me see you," I said eagerly. They floated over to my bed, looking and sounding the same as when I'd seen them all those years ago. The look of love and peace in their bright blue eyes said it all. "I am so very glad to see you again. Will you stay?" I said like a big child.

"We never left you. We helped you as much as you asked us to, and we even helped with some small things that you were too stubborn to ask for. We have never left your side and we never will," they assured me.

"Thank you," I said. "I could really do with your help because I really need to understand about the vile things that happened to me. I am totally mixed up."

"That's why we are here. We heard your call earlier and we don't want you to give up on us. We will help you understand. We love you and we will protect you."

"I badly need help," I reiterated.

"Get some sleep and we will talk soon. Sleep well." With that the room went dark and I drifted off to sleep.

Chapter 12

The next morning I woke up very early and had a great peace within me, a peace I hadn't felt for a long time. I lay there and wondered if I had really seen the Angels the previous night, or if I had just dreamed of them. Then I thought about the priest and what he had said, and I felt my heart sink.

No, I told myself, no; it wasn't my fault – how could it be? I was only a child and didn't know what was happening. I hadn't told anyone because at the time I didn't like or even understand what was happening. I also feared that people wouldn't believe me, so in time I had blocked it out of my mind and buried it so deep that even *I* didn't believe it had happened.

Even then as an adult I felt shame and fear. I was no longer angry, but I did feel the need to tell someone. The problem was, with the reaction I got from the priest, I wasn't sure if I should ever mention it to anyone again. The question – *did* I have anything to do with it? – went around and around in my head all day.

By that evening I had decided not to let it get to me. I had let it all go before and I could do so again. I had realised what the whole *special* thing was all about, so I would just get on with my life.

I vividly recall that I went off to my bedroom to do some reading and a little meditation, but as hard as I tried I just couldn't let it go. I had arranged to go to Lourdes with my mother in a couple of weeks, and hoped I would find the answer there. But the way I was feeling right then I didn't want to go to Lourdes or anywhere else. I heard myself screaming silently "*Help me, please help me*!" Suddenly a still energy fell all around the room and I felt a presence next to me. I looked around and saw my Angels standing there. They folded their soft, gentle wings around me, and I knew I was safe.

"What is it that is upsetting you so much, my precious soul?" my Guardian Angel asked.

"I'm tired of not understanding why things happen and why I always have something to worry about. Just when things start to go right in my life something else from my past comes and upsets me again," I replied, feeling very sorry for myself.

"Well, let's have a look at what it is that's upsetting you so," they invited.

So I told them about confession and about what the priest had said. "Do you really think you had a part to play in that,

Aidan?" My Angel replied with great kindness.

"I don't know any more. I am so mixed up."

"You, my Dear Soul, are not mixed up, but you are afraid. You are afraid you will have to feel the pain and all the dreadful things that go with those experiences; that you will have to tell this to your family and friends and then explain your innocence."

"You're right," I agreed. "I don't want to feel the pain and I don't want to tell anyone. I don't want their pity. But how can I stop blaming myself?" I asked in desperation.

"I know it is hard on you and I am going to take you back to that time and place just for a few moments. You will be safe. I am beside you. Now close your eyes and feel yourself going back, travelling back in time to that classroom… When you look to the top of the room you see yourself and the teacher. Tell me what you see," my Angel said.

"The room is dark, the blinds are closed. He's standing over me with one hand on me, the other in his pocket." My voice was low and shaky and I felt very apprehensive.

"Don't be fearful. Now, what are you doing? Look at the little boy."

I looked at this little boy. The boy is me, a very young child, and he has no concept of what is happening.

"What do you see?" The Angel asked.

"An innocent child," I answered.

"Yes, exactly: an innocent child. Is he asking the man to do this to him?"

"No, not at all. He just wants to leave and he is very upset," I said. "I really want to give him a big hug. He's so afraid and so alone."

"Now could this be your fault in any way?" My Angel asked.

"I know it's not, but it's that seed of doubt that people sow; do you understand?" I really wanted this sorted.

Then they put this question to me: "If you saw your niece or nephew of eight or nine standing at the top of that classroom being abused by that teacher, would you blame them? Would you think they had any part to play in it and would you think them dirty?"

"No, no, no!" I exclaimed. "I would want to protect and love them more and do everything in my power to help them. They are only innocent children and they don't understand."

"So why are you so hard on yourself and why can't you see that it's the same for you?" they probed.

"You've shown me how to look at this in a completely different way and I'll work on this. Thank you. But I will never understand why God would let this happen." I was still confused about this aspect of it.

"Are children not the purest and most special gift God gives to mankind?" they asked.

"Yes; they are pure souls who bring great light into this sometimes dark world."

"And do you think for a moment that God doesn't feel the pain of abuse? He is also very sad when He sees man's in-humanity to man. It hurts Him also. Does God not dwell within us? Well, if so, then why would you think He wouldn't feel this pain? Remember always that God dwells within each and every one of us. You went through a lot in your young life and you will understand why all this happened to you very soon. And you will help others with all your knowledge. Don't be afraid. It will all fall into place in Divine Timing."

It was my first time to hear the words "Divine Timing", but they were to become my favoured and sometimes my most challenging words. The Angels were back and from that day to this I see and talk to them every day. They are a huge part of my everyday life and I do all my healing work through them.

Chapter 13

I always said my journey of understanding and awaking started during a visit to Lourdes. However, my Angels assured me that it had started long before that and it was my *spiritual* soul journey I was now beginning. Life felt fresh and good again. I was better able to control the emotions and pain caused by the abuse I'd suffered. I began to realise this was now in the past – a past that I had no control over. I needed to stop reliving it.

I now had hope and felt strongly that I had a far better future ahead of me. I didn't have to be a victim of my past. It was time to get on with my life and I was happy to be alive. Work was going well once more, but something in the back of my mind constantly told me that I needed to be doing something different.

I began to have longer, deeper conversations with my Angels. They were certainly around a lot more and I was no longer afraid of them. They were everywhere and around everyone I saw. I fully realised at this time that very few people could see them. Not many believed in them either. Yet these great Guardians of Love and Light stood beside every single individual – even those who didn't believe. At least two, and sometimes three, shimmering silhouettes of illuminations stood behind and slightly to the side of each person.

These Beings of Light didn't take up any space, nor did they block the way or cause any difficulty when people moved around.

This display of magnificent colour and gracefulness was a sight to behold. I began to realise for the first time in my life just how honoured I was to be given this blessed gift.

I now needed to work with them and to ask them for their help and guidance. To do this I needed to learn more about them and I needed to know what they expected from me. Over a period of several months, every night before I went to bed, or when I had the house to myself, I'd call on my Angels and ask them about themselves.

I wanted to ask them so much and decided I would start with some basic questions. I'd ask them to confirm for me anything I had read in books about them or anything I'd heard. Was I a "Doubting Thomas"? I sometimes wondered. I was still a bit negative, even though I had come a long way. But the Angels were always patient and answered any questions I put to them. Our conversations would go something like this:

"Can I ask you some questions about Angels?"

"You certainly can, my Little Soul. Anything you want to know about us I will tell you," my Guardian Angel would answer.

"What are Angels?"

"We are messengers from God and Beings of positive energy and love, light and healing."

"Why did God create Angels? What is your work?"

"We bring His message to mankind. We bring answers to prayers. We help in times of danger. We care for you during your lifetime and at your time of death. We praise, worship and rejoice in God and His work. We are your link between heaven and earth."

"Is my Guardian Angel more powerful than other Angels?"

"Ah, powerful: that's not a word we use. We are all equal and we all have our own work to carry out. So our work is equally important. Your Guardian Angels work very hard on your behalf and will always try to guide you and make your life easier," he said, looking very pleased with himself.

"You say Guardian Angels: do we have more than one? I know I have more than one Angel around me at times," I replied.

"Yes, you do; you have at least two. Some people may have more, but always two," he said, knowing what I was about to ask. He put his hand up to stop me speaking.

"One Guardian Angel has been with you in every lifetime and a new one comes to you every time your soul is reborn, to help and guide you. I am the one who has walked with you in every lifetime." This Angel always came when I called. He was always dressed in a beautiful soft pink robe, while the others dressed in either pale green or blue robes.

"So," I said, "what are your names? What shall I call you?" I was longing to hear some very biblical names.

"We don't have names. We don't possess any worldly titles. It is you humans who lovingly give us names. This makes you comfortable and it makes it easier for you to call on us. We love the earthy energy and the meaning they carry," he said with a big smile.

"Right, I'll call you Zechariah. I feel that's a strong name and it suits you because you were always very strong when you came to me in my early days. You also made me strong and helped me cope better." I gave a small bow and waited for his reply.

"I shall accept this beautiful name. Do you know the meaning of this name?" he asked.

"No, I don't, but I always loved the name," I said, feeling a little foolish.

"It means 'God has remembered'. How beautiful is that?" he said, very happy.

"That's amazing, and I am so pleased with the meaning, Now I know why I picked it for you. God remembered me and sent you to help me." Shivers ran down my spine at that moment. Turning to my other beautiful Angel, I asked, "What name should I give you? Your energy is gentle and feminine. I will call you Hannah. Is that OK?"

"Yes, I am very pleased. This name means 'Graceful'. Thank you," she said.

"That is also very beautiful. I picked these because they are among my favourite names and I felt they would suit you both and they do."

"Yes, Beloved Soul, they are very beautiful," Zechariah replied.

"There are hundreds of Angels, so do I work with both of you only, or can I ask others for help?" I asked, slightly confused.

Hannah spoke: "There are billions of Angels all eagerly awaiting your call for help. So don't be afraid to work with them and with us. We can all help."

"So when I speak with you, is there

anything else I should be doing?" I asked just to make sure I wasn't being disrespectful to them in any way.

"When you communicate with us we ask that you simply speak to us as you would to your family, friends and loved ones."

"Do you help us without us asking for your help?" I asked.

"This is always a hard one to answer. Generally you must call on us for help and guidance. Because you are beings of free will, it is up to you to ask for this help. If we were to interfere we might prevent you from learning a valuable lesson in life. But if you are in extreme danger, and it is not your time to pass over, and it is the will of God, then we are allowed to intervene." He smiled and nodded. "Your Guardian Angel is always with you. He never leaves your side and walks with you during your entire lifetime. We will help you in times of danger and comfort you in times of illness and mourning. We are that strength and support that comes from within during these hard times. These are the times we assist without asking because these are the times you are often so lost you don't remember to ask. Remember also when you call on God and ask for His help that God will also send us and any other Angels you may need to assist you. God and the Angels love you without question."

"What about the other Angels? How do I work with them? How do I call on them when they don't have names?" I was totally confused at this stage.

"Names! You place so much importance on names and titles on earth. It's simple: all you do is call on the energy of the Angels you need to help in the situation. So if it's to do with work, you call on the Angels of Career to help and guide you through the issue. If you need laughter and fun in your life, you call on the Angels of Joy, and if it's to do with relationships, you call on the Angels of Romance," he replied.

"Oh thank God, that sounds very simple." I said, relieved.

"Yes, always keep it simple. Please keep it so simple that even a child can look and understand. Everything has become so difficult and hard to understand. Church and religions have made God so complicated. People have just given up because they can't feel God's love. Religion often talks of the judgemental God and not of the loving God. This is the God you must find, and you will only find this God in simplicity and love," Zechariah said.

"Where will I find this God? This is the God I have been looking for. This is the God Jesus speaks of, but I haven't found this God yet. Where is He?"

"This God lives in every one of us. God lives in our heart and soul. God is love. When we live in love we live in the energy and presence of God. God's love is unconditional and does not judge. When you open yourself to God's Divine energy and allow it to flow through you, you are doing God's work of giving healing and love to others," he explained.

"What part do Angels play in the healing?" I asked.

"God is the power of all healing and we Angels assist in bringing this Divine healing into the world around you. Angels use their healing energy to touch you on a deeper spiritual and healing level. A healing can be a hug, a smile, a kind word or an act of kindness. It's when you open your heart to others with empathy, love, forgiveness and understanding without judgement."

"Do Angels know everything?" I asked.

"Like humans, Angels are created by God. This means that, like humans, we don't know everything, nor can we answer everything. Angels are also subject to Divine will. This is what we mean when we speak of Divine Timing. It's God that decides, not us. Only God holds all the answers," they replied.

This was the way these conversations would go from day to day. I remember thinking how very accurate and appropriate were the names I'd chosen for my two Angels. These were names I had loved from a very early age. To this day I don't know where I heard them and why they were always there in my head. It also made a lot of sense to me that they don't have names apart from the ones we give them. I never called out their names when I needed them to help me. I remember calling for God and His Angels to come to help me. I do remember my mam telling me that my Guardian Angel had the same name as me, but I had stopped using it a long time ago. These names, Zechariah and Hannah, seemed to fit my two beautiful Angels perfectly.

I was also introduced by my Angels to my Spirit Guide. He told me his name was Jack. He was a small, stocky, elderly black man who gave me the biggest, warmest hug I'd ever had. His energy was more solid than the

Angels'. It was more grounded, and when he spoke his voice sounded just like ours. While Angels have never lived an earthly existence, Guides have, so they have a deep understanding of all our earthly problems.

One night I got into bed and felt myself fall into a most peaceful and restful sleep. At about 3 a.m. I suddenly sat up bed. My two Guardian Angels were standing beside me and the room was covered in mist. They radiated their vibrant energy and I knew something was about to happen. They assured me everything was all right, but I wasn't afraid. I had complete trust in them and I was longing to know what was happening. They took my hands in theirs and I felt their warmth and protection. Then they asked me to close my eyes and told me they were taking me on a short journey and not to open my eyes until they said so.

My whole body tingled with excitement. As I sat in my bed I rose out of my physical body. I felt light and free and at total peace.

I could feel myself float and it felt good. After a few minutes I was told to open my eyes. I was speechless. They had taken me to a glorious meadow of lush green grass and yellow daisies. A forest, which stood at the foot of a mountain, looked almost barren compared to the meadow. The air was fresh with a warm gentle breeze, which carried that familiar scent of the Angels: sweet pea on a summer's evening. It felt good, but I still didn't know why we were there.

"Do you not recognise this peaceful place? This is your sacred place – your place of healing and your place of perfect peace, your holy place, your God space," they said.

"This is mine?" I asked.

"Yes, Little Soul, this is your place, your sacred place. No one but you, your Angels, your Guides and your God can enter this space. Here in this quiet space of stillness and silence you will move beyond the limitations of your physical body and reconnect with the healing energy of the Divine Master. Fill your heart and soul with this pure love and pure light and, in accepting this, your light will naturally shine stronger and brighter." Zechariah bowed gently and smiled.

"Yes, I will accept this beautiful gift," I said.

"So, my dear child, you can visit this place anytime. All you need to do is close your eyes and call on us and we will take you beyond the physical to this place of perfect peace. In times to come this is the place you will travel to during your healings," Zechariah said.

I didn't reply. I couldn't believe how beautiful everything was. It was all so bright, clean, fresh and invigorating.

"Let's go back. You have had a long, busy day. We shall return again," he said.

I took their hands and within moments I could feel myself connect back into my earth body and I was safe in my bed. My Angels stood at my bedside as I fell back into a deep sleep.

Chapter 14

One day, not long after that experience, I decided to go for a walk. My Angels were very quiet and Jack, my Guide, who never stopped talking on a normal day, had few words. This rare silence bothered me and I asked if I had done something wrong. But they assured me everything was OK.

We walked for another few minutes when, in the distance, I heard a thud and the screech of what sounded like car brakes. Then I saw a blue van travelling at great speed about thirty metres ahead of me. It looked as if there was something trapped under it and being dragged at God knows what speed. Was it an animal or a roll of something? I wondered. The van was swerving all over the road and I felt afraid. The street seemed empty except for a car following behind the van.

I heard myself shouting "Stop, Stop!" but the driver didn't. A tiny bundle escaped from under the van and lay like a ragdoll, limp and lifeless, on the side of the road. I was still a little distance away, but the couple driving behind had stopped. As I ran along the road I saw a *multitude* of Angels gather around the spot. Finally I got to where lay the body of a small girl of about eight years old, with long blonde hair, still holding on tightly to her little bag of sweets.

The lady from the car held one hand while I bent down and held the other. All around the little child gathered the Angels, in great light, attending to her and holding her. Then from behind her came a radiant purple light and from within that light came the most beautiful Angel, shimmering in many colours. I stepped away from the child. I had never seen or witnessed this powerful energy before or experienced such great gentleness and strength.

He appeared in a mighty beam of light – tall, youthful, bearded – and his radiant energy extended way beyond any other Angel I had come in contact with. All the Angels stepped aside for him and he made his way to the stricken child. He bent down, gently embraced the little girl and kissed her on both cheeks; first the right one and then left. Then he held her in his energy for a couple of minutes. Her energy changed, the tension went from her and she became relaxed. The mighty Angel gently took her hand and the spirit of the child left her body and a shining white light radiated all around her. He took the child in his arms, stepped back into the beam of purple light, and they slowly faded away.

"That's good; she felt no pain. She was smiling a little," Jack said reassuringly.

"That Angel, who is he? I have never met his energy before." I said, in shock and awe at the accident and all I had witnessed.

"This is the Divine-like energy called Metatron. He is the one who protects and guides children in life and beyond. She is safe now," Jack replied.

"Why did she die so young? She's so beautiful. It doesn't seem fair to me," I said, still shaken to my core at what I had witnessed.

"It was her time. She had learned all she came to learn and her death was her last lesson. She will need time to adjust now, as indeed will her loved ones here." Hannah replied gently.

Although Metatron had left with the spirit and the soul of the child, the other Angels still protected her body until the ambulance people arrived. They attended to the little girl very carefully and with the greatest respect as they took her body to the hospital.

I was in deep shock for a couple of days after that. It was a terrible experience on a human level, but what a comforting and inspirational sight to see the Angels attend to her and stay with her. And then to witness the great gentleness and love of that powerful Angel, Metatron.

This gave me great comfort in the days that followed. To see a young child die because of reckless driving caused me to question everything at a very deep level. All the while my Angels and Jack reassured me that there *is* a Divine Plan to all our lives and that everything happens for a reason. But still it was very difficult to accept. I knew also that I had been very privileged to be allowed to witness a soul making the transition from this earthly dimension to the heavenly realms.

I can now look back on my life of trials and

challenges with gratitude for all that I have learned and for all that I can share with others. I no longer look back with regrets or blame, as it serves no purpose. Feelings of regret and anger will only make you bitter and twisted and will leave you stuck in the pain and resentment of the past. I am surrounded with love and give thanks daily for this wonderful gift. My life is blessed with a great circle of family and friends and my beloved, wise mother taught me at a very young age just what unconditional love really was. She showed me daily that unconditional love never judges or looks for anything in return. She was, is, and always will be, my greatest Guide.

Questions and Answers

I have asked the Angels many questions that
I myself have been asked. I would like to
share with you some of the answers that I
received on: love, the global economy, the
healing of the planet, death, money, abuse,
evil, forgiveness, the elderly, and how to
work with Angels. It is my hope that by
doing this exercise I can share with you
some of the wisdom that these wonderful
beings want us to understand.

What are Angels and where do they come from?

God created the Angelic realm as he did mankind. Angels are beings of positive energy and pure love and light.

What do Angels do?

We assist in every aspect of your life. We are your direct link between heaven and earth. We care for you during your life and in death. We are the guardians of your well-being and a light for all that is positive, good and true.

Do Angels know everything?

No, we don't. We too are a creation of God and subject to Divine Will. Only God holds all the answers.

How do we communicate with you?

When you wish to communicate with us, simply call on us and we will gently come to your assistance. Speak to us as you would to your beloved family or a dear friend.

When we ask you a question, how should we ask?

Ask clearly for what it is you desire and we will assist, direct and guide you to the best result, provided it is of positive energy and for your highest good and for the good of all concerned.

Why do you not interfere?

If we were to interfere we could prevent you from learning many life lessons and this in turn could alter your free will. Remember you chose to come to this planet to exercise your free will, so we can help you and guide you, but it is you who make the final choice.

Are there Angels for everything?

Yes, there are Angels for everything and every situation in your life and there are millions upon millions of us. There are Angels of Love, Romance, Finance, Career, Health, Fun, Protection, and we could go on and on.

What about dark Angels? Is there such a thing?

There are no such things as dark Angels. Darkness comes from human fear and human fear comes from lack of God, and from greed, dishonesty, cruelty and abuse. Angels are of light and do not know darkness. We come from pure God light and we radiate with the God light of love and healing every time you call on us or even think of us. Our protective loving energy is always by your side. Light will always outshine the darkness and love will always outshine fear, so think and feel the loving light of God at all times and know that you too are filled with the light and love of God.

How do we call on Angels? Do you have names?

No, we don't have names: it is mankind that gave us names. They put earth names on certain energies of Angels who constantly visit the earth, such as Michael, Gabriel and Raphael, to name but a few. These Angels, and indeed all Angels, love and respect the energy of the name you place on them. So it is not necessary to know names: just call on the Angels of Love, or the Angels of Career, or the Angels of Healing, and a conclave of Angels will come and assist you in the situation you find yourself in.

Do we all have a Guardian Angel?

Yes, you all have at least two Guardian Angels. One Guardian Angel has been with you in every lifetime and a second and new Guardian Angel is assigned to you every time your soul is reborn.

They come to help and guide you and to make your life path easier. Your Guardian

Angel is always with you, never leaving your side, and walks with you during your entire lifetime on this planet. We will help you in times of danger and comfort you in times of illness and mourning. We are that strength and support that comes from within during these hard times. These are the times we assist without asking because during these times you are often so lost you don't remember to ask.

Remember also, when you call on God and ask for His help, God will also send us to assist you and any other Angels you may need at that time. God and the Angels love you, and all mankind, without question.

Before your soul is reborn to an earthly body, it meets on the higher planes with other souls that are part of your soul group. Your Guardian Angels and Guides are also there to decide the path and the lessons your soul needs to learn in this lifetime. Then God embraces your soul and fills it with the pure white light of life and the soul starts to journey to earth. It then moves through the different heavenly rays of light, wisdom and knowledge before it is placed in your mother's womb and here you start to adjust to the earth energy again. Your Guardian Angels and your mother's Guardian Angels stand side by side until the day you are born, watching over you and nurturing you.

Many people are afraid of death and of dying. This is what the Angels tell us:

Dearest ones, please do not be afraid of death; we will prepare you for this great journey. For a period of time prior to your passing, your body and soul travel to the Crystal Temple of preparation. Here, in this great Temple of Light, you will become reacquainted with your loved ones who have already passed over and you will become steadily attuned to the lighter God energy you have travelled to. You will become a child of both worlds for this blessed time and this is why so many people speak of loved ones who have passed before they themselves journey to the land of eternal love and light. Be not afraid of death, for beyond this earth awaits a beautiful place of perfect peace. This is a place of reunions. Here you are not judged by what you did or didn't do on earth, but are asked what you have learned. Life is a path of learning and we all choose to learn certain lessons each lifetime. The God that creates you loves you with unconditional love. Unconditional love does not judge or condemn.

What about miscarriages, stillborn babies and sudden infant death?

Before a soul is born it gets together with its soul family and soul group on the great heavenly planes. Here they plan out their life together on earth. Within this soul family, the infant soul then chooses the parents they wish to be with and every soul within that group decides the part they will play on that journey.

There can be a number of reasons why a child chooses to return to heaven early. It could be that the young soul wants to experience a pregnancy or miscarriage. It could be that they themselves didn't feel they were ready to be born, that they felt they didn't have enough knowledge to carry out the lessons they agreed to learn. Perhaps they hadn't fully recovered from the trauma of their previous life. It could also be that they needed to bring the family closer together or to bring them to God/spiritual awareness.

Whatever the lesson is, it is never to bring guilt or unhappiness to the parents. Always remember this precious and wonderful soul chose you to be their soul parents, so in time this soul will always return to you. Mothers, never blame yourself for this event. Even if you were to cover yourself in cotton wool and stay in bed, this precious and perfect soul would still have chosen to leave and return when they were ready. This soul will always return to its soul family. It's important to remember that it is the soul that returns – not the body.

What is love?

My beloved ones, you cannot touch love, but you can be touched by an act of love. You cannot buy love, but you can give it freely. Love is the light of God and God is love. God's love is unconditional and seeks only the good in man.

Love is that smile you give a loved one or a stranger when they look tired or down and need a smile. It's a friendly greeting or a helping hand. Love is being trustworthy and truthful. It's about giving and not expecting anything in return. You can say no and set boundaries and be honest about what you have to say, but always say it with love; for to love is to allow the light and healing love of God to shine in your heart and soul. Be that light of love and healing that burns and illuminates the darkness of war and greed that has shadowed your world. You, my dear children, were created from love to be loved and to give love. Without love, nothing would grow or flourish.

Every day, people ask me about the planet. This is the answer the Angels gave me:

The blessed planet, Mother Earth, is being destroyed before your very eyes. You have raped and murdered this beautiful planet that God so lovingly created for you. You replaced God with ego as you cut down her forests, drained her flood lands, robbed her of almost all her resources, poisoned the seas and skies and then filled and choked the earth with concrete until it could breathe no more. This is what you humans carry out in the name of "progress", and for financial gain. Then you ask why Mother Earth is rebelling, why storms and disasters happen. When you and your leaders step back and see the pain and loss these terrible storms bring, you then ask, "Why?" Still not wanting to take responsibility, you ask, "How could God let this happen?" Again we tell you it is not the work of God but of man and his free will.

Honour the land and its beauty; give thanks daily for everything Mother Earth provides for you, but do not over-use or dry up her resources. Allow her to rest, breathe and be replenished and then she will sustain you and all living things as God intended.

You are all called to live in harmony with Mother Earth and respect all living things. Every day you use and abuse the resources she has provided for you without giving it a thought; you have become careless and wasteful. Be mindful of your actions, dearest children, and remember planet Earth is a sacred place. Be gentle, loving and respectful when you walk this precious ground. If you take responsibility for your own actions, you too can play your part in healing Mother Earth. Invite the Angels of Nature to walk the earth and to bring with them their sacred healing essences so that it may grow and breathe again. Ask the Angels to bring love, light, healing and wisdom to Mother Earth and all of her inhabitants.

Many times I have been asked what the Angels have to say about the global economy and the cause of this global unrest. So I put the question to them.

My dear children, the cause of all this global upset and unrest is basic greed. You have replaced moral values with career, property, selfishness and the desire for material goods. You have turned your back on the poor, the elderly, the hungry, and on God. This is not due to God; it is due to the lack of God in your everyday life and in your dealings with one another. It's about the immoral values you choose to accept and teach to each other. The old way of doing things and the old systems don't work anymore. You must learn to see and do things differently. You now need to learn from your mistakes and rise to a new vibration of awareness and understanding.

People are afraid to ask for money, so I asked the Angels if it wrong to ask.

Dear ones, no, it is not wrong to ask for money or to have money. Money is just an energy of exchange. It is the misuse of this energy and the immoral things that people do to gain more and more money that is wrong. Do not hoard money and do not let it rule your life or be ruled by it. When you live for money alone, you live in the coldness of want. In this energy you will always want and want and want and never have enough; nor will you find happiness. Money doesn't buy happiness. Unhappiness comes from something missing in your life. Happiness can only be found in your heart; it is God that is your real source, not money. God will provide money if you ask and understand your need for it. Money is a good energy and there is nothing wrong with having money. It can improve your life if you manage it wisely and treat it with respect and use it for your higher good. Call on the Angels of Finance when you have money problems and they will come on their golden ray of light to assist and guide you no matter how big or small your financial needs are. You see, my dear children, money is not necessarily the root of all evil. It is how you choose to use your money and how you view the energy of money that makes the difference.

What are Guides?

Your Spirit Guides, unlike Angels, have lived on earth, living many lives. They have learned all of life's lessons and so have become the perfect soul. They come as great teachers to guide and inspire you lovingly along life's path.

What about our parents – are they chosen for us?

My blessed children, you choose your parents; your parents don't choose you. You choose your parents for all the positive things they give you in your life, not for the negative things they carry. Please don't dwell on the negative things they have passed on to you, choose to see them as the challenges that are set before you to draw on your strengths and weaknesses. Sometimes they don't know how to deal with the insecurities and behavioural traits that they exhibit, so they try to unload them on to you, their dear children. Always try to remember that your parents do the best they can with the knowledge that they have at that time and moment.

How do you know when you're with the right partner?

My dear, dear children, when your eyes never tire of seeing, when your heart beats in great joy at the thought of them and when your soul rests in peace, knowing that you are safe and happy in this blessed relationship. My beloved children, rest assured that when you are with the right soul partner you will never have to ask this question or ask for anyone's approval. You will never ask: is it right? Your great gift of knowing within your heart and the joy and relaxation within your soul will reassure you that this is the right soul for you and the God-given person.

Why do people suffer illness?

My beloved children, illness is not a punishment and it is wrong to believe God must be angry with you. It always has meaning and it is always about growth, and sometimes that growth may be incredibly difficult to detect and understand. You are not expected to understand illness and pain, and it is human and acceptable to feel angry with God during this time. In human terms there are no words to explain why illness occurs; it is between God and the individual. Only God holds the answer to this question and, like everything else in your life, you choose and accept to learn different lessons each time you begin your journey to earth. Remember God loves each one of us unconditionally and this love is constant and without limitations.

Can Angels change our life path?
No, dear ones, we can't change your life path. This is something you chose before you came to earth and you are in control of your own life and how you might live it. It's only your free will and stubbornness that can change your life path. We hold the map and the direction of your great journey in every lifetime. However, we can help and guide you along your life path and make your journey easier and more fulfilling. So when you feel lost or confused on this great journey of life, call on us. We will help clear

away your confusion and lovingly guide you along your true path.

Can we ask our Angels for something and get the opposite?

My precious souls, we will always strive to give you what you ask for, if it's for your higher good and the good of all concerned. We would never send you the opposite if it meant it would bring you pain or upset. If we don't send what you ask for, we will always send you something equally good in its place. Your prayers and requests will never go unheard; trust us and follow our directions – we will never lead you astray.

When we ask for Angels' help, do they take this request to God or do they work alone?

Always remember everything comes from God; therefore anything you ask of us comes through God and from God. We Angels act as a mediator between God and you, His beloved earth souls. We never work alone; we always work with the Divine Will and love of God. Only God holds the power to grant your request.

When asking the Angels for a favour, do we ask once or should we keep asking until we're sure that you receive our request?

Ask as often as you wish, my dear children, but once is quite sufficient. When you ask, we will immediately take your request to the eternal love and light of God. Just have faith and leave it in our hands and don't worry, we will never forget anything you ask for in love. Just stand back and wait: we will give you guidance.

When Angels answer our prayers, how should we thank them?

This, my dear soul, is so very simple. Just sit in stillness and silent prayer asking us to gather round you and then simply and clearly say, "Thank you for your help, support and direction." In thanking us you are also thanking God. Two little words that mean so much to us and to so many earth people, but these beautiful God-filled words are not used often enough. Please use them more and fill the earth with the God energy that they carry. Make them a part of your everyday life, starting from today.

What if I make a request and I do not get it?

This is a case of God knows best. You often ask for things for selfish reasons or something that may not benefit you or your life in any way. So God in His greater wisdom may not grant it or send it to you on that occasion. Always accept the will and love of God as it is for your higher good and the good of all concerned in those particular circumstances.

Many people don't want to know about their Angels and don't believe in them. What should we believers do?

My dear earth children, that is their choice and don't allow it to affect your thoughts and knowing. If they choose not to work with us, we will still stand by them. In time, should they choose to call or look for us, we will be there to help and guide them on their way. Should they choose not to, their abilities will be limited.

How do I invite Angels into my life?

This, my dear ones, is the easiest thing you will ever have to do. Sit in silent meditation and invite us in. We will lose no time in coming. Then simply speak to us, as you would do to your best friend. At first you may not feel our presence or hear our words, but in time you will become familiar with our energy and vibration. You may feel a change in the room temperature, the delicate smell of a scented flower, the flicker of a light or a sense of knowing that someone is present. The energy will always be light and comforting. Please do not allow fear to block you from making this contact with us. Never be afraid: we won't reveal ourselves until you are truly ready and comfortable with us.

Which religion is nearest to God?

All religion is near God and all religion is far away from God also. Every religion believes it is the true follower of God and holds the true messages of God. Many religions have man-made rules that are not of God but of power and control. Your place of birth and your culture usually determine which religion you are given or choose to take up. God is love, and love is the key to growth, acceptance and understanding. Let all religions work on what they have in common and not what keeps them apart. The love of God is what each and every religion has in common, and ego is what keeps them apart.

Why should we forgive?

You can choose to forgive in order to grow spiritually and physically. Forgiveness is the greatest gift you can give yourself and your enemies. It holds the power and the energy of freedom and peace. Forgiveness allows a new chapter of your life to begin and it gives you permission to move on in love by letting go of pain and hurt.

What about abuse? Why does God let it happen?

There are many forms of abuse: physical, emotional, sexual, political, employment and religious, to name but a few. They are all centred on having control, taking control and ultimately trying to overpower another person, race, country, etc. Abuse is ego-driven and again is mainly due to a lack of God. The person or people creating the abuse have closed hearts and have shut themselves out from God's love and light.

You blame God for allowing abuse, but it is not our beloved God that creates or allows this. Remember you are living on a planet of free will, so it is man's inhumanity to man and the need for power and control that cause abuse. God weeps to see such things happen. You must take responsibility for your own free will and actions and try to look for new ways to deal with these abusers and protect the weak and innocent.

What is abundance?

My dear children, most people think in terms of financial gain when they talk about abundance. However, it means different things to different people and it is far more than money and wealth. Abundance covers the areas of health, wealth, happiness, emotional and spiritual awareness and perfect self-expression. Having enough in your life is your abundance; you will never need any more than enough to live a happy, safe and balanced life. Abundance is not about storing and hoarding vast amounts of anything: that is just greed and it shows a lack of trust in our Heavenly Father. Give thanks daily for all the wonderful things already in your life and this small blessing will create more. Bring your awareness to all that is currently present in your life and you will understand that you are already abundant.

What happens to people who commit suicide?

Remember, my children, God doesn't judge our loved ones who have committed suicide. They are as welcome in heaven as any other human that leaves your planet. We Angels come to their aid and take special care of these beautiful souls and guide them to the light in loving care and understanding. Please do not fear for them or think they will be punished in any way. They are loved unconditionally and taken to the master house of healing. Here we enfold them lovingly in our wings and bring them complete healing and perfect peace. They rest in love, light and peace.

Talk to us about the elderly.

My beloved children, your once golden rule of caring for and respecting your old and infirm has sadly passed. You have cast your elderly aside, making them feel lonely, isolated and useless and a burden to their families and society. But these great people have made their mark on life. They have worked hard under very difficult conditions. They have fought cruel and terrible wars to make your world a safer and better place to live in. They have a wealth of love, wisdom and information to share with you, so please don't turn your backs on them. Listen and learn from these great masters of knowledge. They have earned your love and respect. Growing old is not a disease, it is part of the human cycle and a process that will come to you all one day. It is a part of the life cycle that you should honour and cherish. Embrace your elderly and care for them by giving them back their rightful place in society and allowing them to grow old with dignity and grace. Age is not a burden, age is honourable.

Why can't all of us see Angels, even though we ask and are very keen to meet our Guardian Angels?

My dearest children, your fear is what keeps us from presenting ourselves to you, and our knowing that you are not yet ready for this joyous and powerful meeting. We will show ourselves to you when you grow and become more spiritually developed and have formed a personal and trusting relationship with your Angels. Always remember that the human way has always been "Seeing is believing", whereas the spiritual way is "Believe and you will see".

How do Angels send us messages?

We send you messages in many ways that are comfortable and fitting for you, such as a small white feather, a gentle breeze on your cheek, finding a coin in an unusual place, a gentle voice in your head saying beautiful and encouraging things or what you humans describe as a "gut feeling". These are our most frequent methods of sending messages to you and this is to let you know that we are around you, protecting and loving you. We send messages to you all the time, messages of hope and inspiration.

Sometimes we speak through other people – like friends, family or even that stranger you talk to at the bus stop who will inspire you and uplift your heart. It can at times be the message in that book that falls from the shelf and, when you read from it, it touches your heart in a special way or answers one of your most important questions. Perhaps at times it is the messages in the song you hear, the poem you have read, a photo or a gift that someone gives you. There are so many ways in which we try to communicate daily. Sadly, because of your human conditioning you sometimes fail to see the simplicity in our way of speaking to you. Our messages will always be very positive and never make you feel uncomfortable or uneasy.

Why are so many marriages breaking up?

My beloved children, the universe is going through a massive energy transformation and many of the emotional issues that humans hold are being brought to the surface. This can cause great difficulty within relationships that were initially made in the name of love, but that were really built on insecurity and neediness within the individual.

If you marry the wrong person, are you bound to stay with them because of the vows you took?

My dear children, there is no such thing as marrying the wrong person. Nothing in your universe happens without purpose. You are drawn to the perfect person in every situation to help teach you more about yourself. Relationships help you question more about who you are and to look at new ways to grow through your experiences. If you did not know hate, how would you know love? If you did not experience darkness, how would you know light? Life is all about learning; that is what your planet is about – the great school of learning – and this is what your soul chooses to experience. Relationships, in whatever manner they present themselves, are a great opportunity of learning through your emotions.

Remember, nothing is carved in stone. You must believe you have choice in everything you do, so therefore you cannot blame "vows" for your unhappiness. You have to take responsibility for yourself and choose what is best for you.